D1526956

What Are
Mountains?

by Lisa Trumbauer

Consulting Editor: Gail Saunders-Smith, Ph.D.

Consultant: Sandra Mather, Ph.D., Professor Emerita,
Department of Geology and Astronomy,
West Chester University
West Chester, Pennsylvania

Pebble Books

an imprint of Capstone Press
Mankato, Minnesota

Pebble Books are published by Capstone Press
151 Good Counsel Drive, P.O. Box 669, Mankato, Minnesota 56002
http://www.capstone-press.com

1 2 3 4 5 6 07 06 05 04 03 02

Library of Congress Cataloging-in-Publication Data
Trumbauer, Lisa, 1963–
    What are mountains? / by Lisa Trumbauer.
    p. cm. —(Earth features)
    Includes bibliographical references and index.
    ISBN 0-7368-0989-9
    1. Mountains—Juvenile literature. [1. Mountains.] I. Title. II. Series.
GB512 .T78 2002
551.43′2—dc21   2001000268

Summary: Simple text and photographs introduce mountains and their features.

Note to Parents and Teachers

The Earth Features series supports national science standards for units on landforms of the earth. The series also supports geography standards for using maps and other geographic representations. This book describes and illustrates mountains. The photographs support early readers in understanding the text. The repetition of words and phrases helps early readers learn new words. This book also introduces early readers to subject-specific vocabulary words, which are defined in the Words to Know section. Early readers may need assistance to read some words and to use the Table of Contents, Words to Know, Read More, Internet Sites, and Index/Word List sections of the book.

A mountain is much taller than the land around it.

foothills

Foothills are small
mountains at the base
of a mountain.

summit

A summit is the top
of a mountain.

Tall mountains have snow at the summit.

A mountain range is
a group of mountains.

Some mountains
have pointed summits.

Some mountains
have rounded summits.

18

Some mountains
are volcanoes.

Mount McKinley

North America

Mount McKinley is in Alaska. It is the tallest mountain in North America.

Words to Know

base—the bottom of a mountain

foothill—a small mountain or hill at the base of a large mountain

pointed—sharp and jagged

range—a chain or large group of mountains

summit—the very top of a mountain; many summits are covered with snow.

volcano—a mountain with vents; a vent is a long, narrow passage that goes deep into the earth; melted rock, ash, and gases erupt through the vents.

Read More

Chambers, Catherine. *Mountains.* Mapping Earthforms. Chicago: Heinemann Library, 2000.

Dwyer, Jackie. *Mountains.* Nature Books. New York: PowerKids Press, 2000.

Fowler, Allan. *Living in the Mountains.* Rookie Read-about Geography. New York: Children's Press, 2000.

Jennings, Terry. *Mountains.* Restless Earth. Parsippany, N.J.: Silver Burdett Press, 1998.

Internet Sites

BrainPOP: Volcanoes
http://www.brainpop.com/science/earth/volcanoes/index.weml

Denali for Kids
http://www.pbs.org/wgbh/nova/denali/kids

Images of the Canadian Rockies
http://www.frontrange.ab.ca/Media

World Records in Earth Science
http://www.extremescience.com/earthsciport.htm

Index/Word List

Word Count: 70
Early-Intervention Level: 14

Editorial Credits
Martha E. H. Rustad, editor; Kia Bielke, cover designer and illustrator;
    Kimberly Danger, photo researcher

Photo Credits
Comstock, Inc., 1
CORBIS, cover, 4, 6, 8, 14
International Stock/Warren Faidley, 18
John Elk III, 10
Photo Network/Karen Lawrence, 16
Visuals Unlimited/John D. Cunningham, 12; Patrick J. Endres, 20